W9-BFO-855

ST PAUL
LIBRARY
ELEMENTARY

PROPERTY OF
NORWALK CITY SCHOOLS
AUXILIARY SERVICES
PURCHASED *Title VI 99-00*

WOODLANDS

BIOMES

Lynn M. Stone

PROPERTY Oi
NORWALK CITY SCHOOLS
AUXILIARY SERVICES
PURCHASED Title VI 99-00

The Rourke Corporation, Inc.
Vero Beach, Florida 32964

ST. PAUL
LIBRARY
ELEMENTARY

00-72

© 1996 The Rourke Corporation, Inc.

All rights reserved. No part of this book
may be reproduced or utilized in any
form or by any means, electronic or
mechanical including photocopying,
recording or by any information storage
and retrieval system without permission
in writing from the publisher.

PHOTO CREDITS
All photos © Lynn M. Stone

Library of Congress Cataloging-in-Publication Data
Stone, Lynn M.
    Woodlands / by Lynn M. Stone.
        p.   cm. — (Biomes)
    Includes index.
    Summary: Briefly describes the different kinds of woodlands in
North America and some of the plants and animals found there.
    ISBN 0-86593-422-3
    1. Forest ecology—Juvenile literature. 2. Forests and forestry—
Juvenile literature. 3. Forest ecology—North America—Juvenile
literature. 4. Forests and forestry—North America—Juvenile
literature. [1. Forests and forestry. 2. Forest ecology.
3. Ecology.] I. Title. II. Series: Stone, Lynn M. Biomes.
QH541.5.F6S77 1996
574.5'2642—dc20   95-46285
                                                                      CIP
                                                                      AC

Printed in the USA

TABLE OF CONTENTS

WOODLANDS

North America's woodlands are big areas covered mostly by trees. Woodlands, or forests, cover much of North America. Wherever soil and weather will let them, woodlands will grow.

In North America, woodlands follow rivers, cover hills, and make mountainsides green.

Along with trees, woodlands have an **understory** (UN der stor ee) of bushes and smaller plants. This mix of woodland plants makes homes for many kinds of wild animals.

A mix of needle-leaved and broad-leaved woodlands follow a river's path in Vermont

KINDS OF WOODLANDS

North America has many kinds of woodlands. Each is named for the kind of trees that grow there. Some trees cannot grow where others can.

Much of eastern North America is covered by trees with wide leaves. These trees lose their leaves each autumn. In other places, woodlands are made up mostly of needle-leaved trees. These trees do not shed their needlelike leaves all at once.

In the Far North, woodlands disappear. The frozen earth — **permafrost** (PER muh frawst) — keeps trees from growing.

Needle-leaved trees — spruces, firs, pines — cover mountains in the West and North

LIFE IN THE WOODLANDS

Woodland plants are food for many animals. The plants themselves grow by making food from sunlight, soil, and water.

Insects, wild turkeys, box turtles, mice, moose, black bears, and squirrels are just a few of the woodland plant-eaters. Some of these animals are **prey** (PRAY) for woodland **predators** (PRED uh torz) — the hunters.

One of the most skillful predators is the silver-furred lynx of the North Woods. The lynx dodges around trees to chase snowshoe rabbits.

ST. PAUL
LIBRARY
ELEMENTARY

The thick-furred lynx prowls woodlands of the Far North

WOODLAND PLANTS

Under the oldest, tallest trees in a woodland are younger trees, bushes, grasses, mosses, mushrooms, and wildflowers. Each spring the wildflower blooms brighten the forest floor.

Some of the most amazing woodlands in North America are those which have never been cut by loggers. These are the **ancient** (AIN chent) old-growth forests.

In California's old-growth forests, some of the redwood trees were alive in the late 1400s, at the same time as Christopher Columbus. The old redwoods are the tallest trees in the world!

Spring wildflowers bloom beneath the still-bare branches of oaks and hickories in Illinois

*California redwoods stand tall in early morning fog
that blankets the state's Pacific coast*

Wild turkeys are the largest of America's woodland birds

BIRDS OF THE WOODLANDS

The woodpecker is a well-known bird of the woodlands because it is often heard, even when it is not seen.

Woodpeckers hammer trees with their beaks. By chipping away bark, woodpeckers find insects. They also drill tree holes for their nests.

Owls are night birds of the woodlands. Their large eyes work well in dim light.

Owl ears hear the softest sounds, even the rustle of a mouse on leaves.

Woodpeckers depend upon forest trees for food and nest holes

MAMMALS OF THE WOODLANDS

Woodlands give some **mammals** (MAM uhlz) a place to hide and find food. Many woodland mammals — squirrels, lynxes, martens, porcupines, raccoons, and black bears — are climbers.

By being able to hurry up a tree, an animal can often avoid danger. The marten, though, hunts red squirrels and birds in the treetops.

Skunks, opossums, foxes, deer, elk, and wolves visit woodlands for sleep and shelter. They do most of their hunting and eating in more open areas.

Slow on the ground, the porcupine finds safety in forest trees

OTHER WOODLAND ANIMALS

The forest floor may seem lifeless, but it's a busy place. Worms, crickets, centipedes, spiders, and slugs live among the leaves. Beetles and other insects hide in the rotting bark of fallen logs.

Toads, mice, and box turtles hunt on the carpet of old leaves. Above them, tree frogs live in the branches. Their chorus of croaks is woodland music on rainy nights in the South.

Box turtles eat both plants and animals that they find on the forest floor

19

VISITING THE WOODLANDS

Everyone enjoys a walk in the woods. Animals may be hard to see, but their signs and sounds are all around.

Deer leave scrape marks on tree bark. **Sapsucker** (SAP suk er) holes ooze sap on tree trunks. Footprints trail across the snow.

The whippoorwill, calling its own name — *whip-poor-will, whip-poor-will!* — signals that night is coming. In darkness, the barred owl makes a deep sound — *who-cooks-for-you, who-cooks-for-you-all?*

20

Visitors often surprise raccoons on woodland trails

PROTECTING THE WOODLANDS

Woodlands are good for people as well as wildlife. People use trees for homes, furniture, paper, and other purposes.

Some woodlands are used for the harvest of trees. Others are saved for wildlife, hiking, and camping.

The U.S. Government owns millions of acres of woodlands in national forests. These lands are used for logging, homes for wildlife, and fun for people.

Some of the finest old-growth woodlands are protected in Redwood National Park and Great Smoky Mountain National Park.

Glossary

ancient (AIN chent) — very old

mammal (MAM uhl) — furry, air-breathing, warm-blooded, milk-producing animals

permafrost (PER muh frawst) — ground frozen year-round

predator (PRED uh tor) — an animal that kills other animals for food

prey (PRAY) — an animal that is killed by another animal for food

sapsucker (SAP suk er) — birds in the woodpecker family that drill holes in trees to get sap

understory (UN der stor ee) — the layer of shrubs and young trees under the forest treetops

INDEX

ST. PAUL
LIBRARY
ELEMENTARY